BOOKS BY W. S. MERWIN

POEMS

The Compass Flower 1977

The First Four Books of Poems (INCLUDING A Mask for
Janus (1952), The Dancing Bears (1954), Green with
Beasts (1956) AND The Drunk in the
Furnace (1960)   1975

Writings to an Unfinished Accompaniment   1973

The Carrier of Ladders   1970

The Lice   1967

The Moving Target   1963

PROSE

Houses and Travellers   1977

The Miner's Pale Children   1970

TRANSLATIONS

Selected Translations 1968–1978

Iphigeneia at Aulis, by Euripedes
(with George E. Dimock, Jr.)   1977

Classical Sanskrit Love Poetry
(with J. Moussaieff Masson)   1977

Vertical Poetry (Poems by Roberto Juarroz)   1977

Osip Mandelstam, Selected Poems
(with Clarence Brown)   1974

Asian Figures   1973

Transparence of the World
(Poems by Jean Follain)   1969

Voices (Poems by Antonio Porchia)   1969

Products of the Perfected Civilization (Selected Writings
of Chamfort)   1969

Twenty Poems of Love and a Song of Despair
(Pablo Neruda)   1969

Selected Translations 1948–1968   1968

The Song of Roland   1963

Lazarillo de Tormes   1962

The Satires of Persius   1961

Spanish Ballads   1960

The Poem of the Cid   1959

W. S. MERWIN

SELECTED TRANSLATIONS 1968-1978

W.S. MERWIN

SELECTED TRANSLATIONS
1968–1978

ATHENEUM
New York

1979

Certain of the translations in this volume have appeared previously as follows:

GREEK: from *Greek Anthology and Other Ancient Greek Epigrams,* edited by Peter Jay, published by Oxford University Press, New York, 1973.

JOAO CABRAL DE MELO NETO: The Man from Up-country Talking; Two of the Festivals of Death; The Drafted Vulture: in *An Anthology of Twentieth-Century Brazilian Poetry,* edited by Elizabeth Bishop and Emanual Brasil, copyright © 1972, published by Wesleyan University Press.

FRANCISCO DE QUEVEDO: Love Constant Beyond Death: in *TriQuarterly.*

PEDRO SALINAS: This iron chain; I can't see you but I know: in *Field.*

VICENTE HUIDIBRO: Poetry Is A Heavenly Crime: in *Doors and Mirrors,* edited by Hortense Carpentier and Janet Brof, copyright © 1972, published by Viking Penguin.

JORGE LUIS BORGES: My Whole Life; To a Minor Poet of the Greek Anthology; The Poet Tells of His Fame: in *Jorge Luis Borges: Selected Poems 1923-1967,* edited by Norman di Giovanni, copyright © 1972, published by Delacorte.

NICANOR PARRA: A Man; Song of the Foreigner: in *Ironwood.*

NICANOR PARRA: I Jehovah Decree; Everything Used to Look Good to Me: in *Doors and Mirrors,* edited by Hortense Carpentier and Janet Brof, copyright © 1972, published by Viking Penguin.

JUAN JOSE ARREOLA: Elegy; The Cave, Telemachus; Deer: in *New Poetry of Mexico,* edited by Octavio Paz and Mark Strand, published by E. P. Dutton & Co., Inc.

ROBERTO JUARROZ: Sometimes my hands wake me up; A man spells out his tiredness; There will come a day: in *The New York Review of Books.*

ROBERTO JUARROZ: If we knew the point: *The New Yorker.*

JAIME SABINES: From Diario Semanario; I have eyes to see; From the bodies; I'm out to find a man: in *Doors and Mirrors,* edited by Hortense Carpentier and Janet Brof, copyright © 1972, published by Viking Penguin.

OSIP MANDELSTAM: all the selections come from *Osip Mandelstam, Selected Poems,* translated by Clarence Brown and W. S. Merwin, published by Atheneum, 1973.

CROW TEXTS: the basis for all the translations will be found in *Crow Texts,* collected, translated, and edited by Robert H. Lowie, copyright © 1960 by The Regents of the University of California, reprinted by permission of the University of California Press.

QUECHUA: Prayer; Prayer; I'm bringing up a fly; When you find you're alone on the island in the river: in *The Hudson Review.*

TZOTZIL: Belly-Ache: in *The New York Review of Books.*

TZELTAL: Story of the Ants and Grasshoppers: in *The Nation.*

ESKIMO: Song of the Old Woman; My song was ready: translated from French versions by Paul Emile Victor, *Poèmes Eskimo,* Seghers, 1958, by permission of the author.

MALGACHE: Bear in mind; Now you're ripe for me: translated from French versions by Jean Paulhan, *Les Hain-Tenys,* Gallimard, 1938.

MALAYAN, KOREAN, JAPANESE and CHINESE FIGURES all come from *Asian Figures,* published by Atheneum, 1973.

SANSKRIT: all from *Classical Sanskrit Love Poetry,* edited by W. S. Merwin and J. Moussaieff Masson, copyright © 1977, published by Columbia University Press. I like sleeping with somebody; Hiding in the/cucumber garden: originally in *East West Journal.*

MIRZA GHALIB: Ghazals V, XII, XXV, and XV: in *Ghazals of Ghalib,* edited by Aijaz Ahmad, copyright © 1971, published by Columbia University Press.

Published simultaneously in Canada by McClelland and Stewart Ltd.
Library of Congress catalog card number 78-55021
ISBN 0-689-10903-2
Manufactured by American Book-Stratford Press, Saddle Brook, New Jersey
Designed by Harry Ford
First Edition

PN
6101
M454

FOR RICHARD HOWARD

FOREWORD

WHEN Pope set out to translate Homer almost everything (as it appears to us) was known beforehand. He knew who most of his immediate readers would be: they had subscribed for the translations. They, in turn, knew—or thought they knew—who Homer was, and they knew the text, in the original. Both the subscribers and the translator took it for granted that the proper form for heroic verse, in English, must of course be the heroic couplet. Pope's work was expected to display the wit, elegance, and brilliance with which he could render a generally accepted notion of the Homeric poems into a familiar English verse form.

Since the 18th century, and especially since the beginning of modernism, more and more translations have been undertaken with the clear purpose of introducing readers (most of them, of course, unknown to the translators) to works they could not read in the original, by authors they might very well never have heard of, from cultures, traditions and forms with which they had no acquaintance. The contrast with Pope's situation is completed by the phenomenon that has appeared with growing frequency in the past half century, of poet-translators who do not, themselves, know the languages from which they are making their versions, but must rely, for their grasp of the originals, on the knowledge and work of others.

New—or different—assumptions mean different risks. New assumptions about the meaning of the word "translation," whether or not they are defined, imply different aspects of the basic risk of all translation, however that is conceived. Which is no risk at all, in the terms of the most common cliché on the subject: that all translation is impossible. We seem to need it, just the same, insofar as we need literature at all. In our time, an individual or social literary culture without it is unthinkable. What is it that we think we need? We begin with the idea that it is the original—which means our relative conception of the original, as scholars, potential translators, or readers. At the outset, the notion is probably not consciously involved with any thought of the available means of translation. The "original" may even figure as something that might exist in more forms than one, just as it can be understood by more than one reader. But if we take a single word of any language and try to find an exact equivalent in another, even if the second language is closely akin to the first, we have to admit that it cannot be done. A single primary denotation may be shared; but the constellation of secondary meanings, the moving rings of associations, the etymological echoes, the sound and its own levels of association, do not have an equivalent because they cannot. If we put two words of a language together and repeat the attempt, the failure is still more obvious. Yet if we continue, we reach a point where some sequence of the first language conveys a dynamic unit, a rudiment of form. Some energy of the first language begins to be manifest, not only in single words but in the charge of their relationship. The surprising thing is that at this point the hope of translation does not fade altogether, but begins to emerge. Not that these rudiments of form in the original language can be matched—any more than individual words could be—with exact equivalents in another. But the imaginative force which they embody, and which single words embody in context, may suggest convocations of words in another language that will have a comparable thrust and sense.

By "rudiments of form" I mean recognizable elements of verbal order, not verse forms. I began with what I suppose was, and perhaps still is, a usual preconception about the latter: that fidelity in translating a poem should include an ambition to reproduce the original verse form. Besides, I started translating partly as a discipline, hoping that the process might help me to

Foreword

learn to write. Pound was one of the first to recommend the
practice to me. I went to visit him at St. Elizabeth's in the '40's,
when I was a student. He urged me to "get as close to the
original as possible," and told me to keep the rhyme scheme of
the poems I was translating, too, if I could, for the exercise as
much as anything else. He was generous. And eloquent about
what the practice could teach about the possibilities of English.
He recommended that I should look, just then, at the Spanish
romancero, and I did; but it was almost fifteen years before I
actually made versions of many of the *romances*—and without
the original rhyme schemes. I kept to his advice, at the time.
When I did come, gradually, to abandon more and more often
the verse forms of poems that I was translating, I did not try to
formulate any precise principle for doing so. Translation is a
fairly empirical practice, usually, and the "reasons" for making
particular choices, however well grounded in scholarship, are
seldom wholly explicable. I would have recognized, probably
quite early, a simple reluctance to sacrifice imagined felicities
of the potential English version, to keep a verse pattern that
was, in a sense, abstract. The preference seems to me practical,
at least. I think I began to consider the subject more systematic-
ally when I was trying to decide on the best form for a transla-
tion of the *Chanson de Roland*. I had before me versions in
blank verse both regular and more or less free, and one which
contrived to keep not only the metrical structure of the Old
French but the rhyme scheme: verse paragraphs known as
laisses, sometimes many lines in length, each line ending with
the same assonance. The result, in English, struck me as nothing
more than an intellectual curiosity; unreadable. The word order
of the lifeless English was contorted, line by line, to get those
sounds to come out right. As for any of the virtues of the ori-
ginal that had moved hearers for centuries and contributed to
the poem's survival over a thousand years, there was scarcely an
indication of what they might have been. It's easy to multiply
examples of this kind of translation. And yet it must be true

that in translating, as in writing, formal verse, exigencies of the form itself occasionally contribute to the tension and resonance of the language. But I realized at some point that I had come to consider the verse conventions of original poems as part of the original language, in which they had a history of associations like that of individual words—something impossible to suggest in English simply by repeating the forms. Verse conventions are to a large degree matters of effects, that depend partly on a familiarity which cannot, of course, be translated at all. The effects of the convention in the new language can never be those it produces in the former one. This is true even with forms that have already been adopted. There would be certain obvious advantages in retaining the sonnet form in English, if translating a sonnet from Italian, but however successful the result, the sonnet form in English does not have the same associations it has in Italian; its effect is not the same; it does not mean the same thing. And sometimes an apparent similiarity of form can be utterly misleading. The *Chanson de Roland*, again, for example. The original is in a ten syllable line, and an English-speaking translator would naturally think, at first, of iambic pentameter. But if the poem is translated into any sort of blank verse in English (leaving aside the question of the relative vitality and brightness of that form in our age) the result is bound to evoke reverberations of the pentameter line in English from Marlowe through Tennyson—echoes that drown the real effect and value of the Old French verse.

I am describing a general tendency drawn from practice and not enunciating a principle. On the other side of the question, I am quite convinced of the impossibility of ever really translating *The Divine Comedy* into any other language, yet I am grateful for several English versions of it, rhymed ones included, for insights into the original, and I recognize that certain of the rhymed translations—for short passages, at least —convey glimpses of what Dante was doing with his highly functional form. But I think that is a recommendation, also, for having many versions, by different hands, of a given poem. And if I had to choose one translation of Dante, it would be "literal", and in prose.

The whole practice is based on paradox: wanting the original leads us to want a translation. And the very notion of making or using a translation implies that it will not and cannot be the original. It must be something else. The original assumes the status of an impossible ideal, and our actual demands must concern themselves with the differences from it, with the manner of standing in stead of it. When I tried to formulate practically what I wanted of a translation, whether by someone else or by me, it was something like this: without deliberately altering the overt meaning of the original poem, I wanted the translation to represent, with as much life as possible, some aspect, some quality of the poem which made the translator think it was worth translating in the first place. I know I arrived at this apparently simple criterion by a process of elimination, remembering all the translations—whatever their other virtues—that I had read, or read at, and set down, thinking "if the original is really *like* that, what could have been the point of translating it?"

The quality that is conveyed to represent the original is bound to differ with different translators, which is both a hazard and an opportunity. In the ideal sense in which one wants only the original, one wants the translator not to exist at all. In the practical sense in which the demand takes into account the nature of translation, the gifts—such as they are— of the translator are inescapably important. A poet-translator cannot write with any authority using someone else's way of hearing.

I have not set out to make translations that distorted the meaning of the originals on pretext of some other overriding originality. For several years I tried to maintain illogical barriers between what I translated and "my own" writing, and I think the insistence on the distinction was better than indulging in a view of everything being the (presumably inspired) same. But no single thing that anyone does is wholly separate from any other, and impulses, hopes, predilections toward writings as yet unconceived certainly must have manifested themselves in the choices of poems from other languages that I preferred to read and wanted to translate, and in the ways that I went about both. And whatever is done, translation included, obviously has some effect on what is written afterwards. Except in a very few cases it would be hard for me to trace, in subsequent writings of my own, the influence of particular translations that I have made, but I know that the influences were and are there. The work of translation did teach, in the sense of forming, and making available, ways of hearing.

Re-examining and choosing the collection that was to be published as *Selected Translations 1948–1968* provided a natural occasion for reviewing what I thought I had been trying to do, and for considering what relation future translations of mine might conceivably bear to their originals. Since then I have tended, at least part of the time, toward a greater freedom from the original verse conventions, with a view to suggesting some vitality of the original in forms native to English. The tendency was not altogether new, and has not been consistent. It was more like the recognition of a curiosity than a decision. In translating several modern poets from French and Spanish— Follain, Sabines—where the forms of the originals seemed to bear affinities with what is most hopeful in contemporary American poetry, I tried to suggest the original cadences as closely as I could. I had come to feel that one function of translation was to extend what could be said and heard in the new language—as original writing would do—but I was not anxious to conclude that there was only one way of doing so. I had been reading, for instance, Budge's translations of Egyptian Pyramid texts, and had been struck by how much more life—and to my way of hearing it, poetry—there was in the transliterations, hieroglyph by hieroglyph, than in the ver-

sion Budge had edited into "good English." I wanted to leave
some of the habits of English prose word order in abeyance, to
see just how necessary they might or might not be, and find
new tensions by other means—a process as old as poetic con-
vention itself, a displacement of old forms with the elements of
new ones. In the translations in *Asian Figures* I let the sequence
of the ideograms (which in most cases I had in front of me,
with their transliterations) suggest the English word order,
where that could be done without destroying the sense. One
object in working with three sonnets of Quevedo's was to have
the Spanish baroque phrasing evoke some of the same gnarled
diction in English, and to echo the movement, the dramatic
development of the sonnet form, but not the form itself. The
series of translations from Ghalib, made from literal versions,
scholarly material, and direct guidance supplied by Aijaz
Ahmad, were part of the same impulse. My first drafts remained
close to the original *ghazal* form, and both Aijaz and I thought
them papery. As he planned to include in the eventual publica-
tion the original texts, literal versions, and his notes on vocabu-
lary, the whole point of the enterprise was to produce
something else from the material—poems in English, if possible.
The rule was that they were not to conflict with Ghalib's
meaning, phrase by phrase, but that they need not render
everything, either. Translation was viewed as fragmentary in
any case; one could choose the fragments, to some degree.
Considering the inadequacy of any approach to translation, I
had been thinking of Cézanne's painting the Montagne St.
Victoire over and over, each painting new, each one another
mountain, each one different from the one he had started to
paint. I imagined that in translating a poem something might
be gained by making a series of versions bringing out different
possibilities. I still think so, though I realize that versions, how-
ever many, from a single poet-translator are likely to sound
like variants of each other, and echo the translator's ear at least
as clearly as they do the original.

The Ghalib translations are among those made without any first-hand knowledge of the original language, as I have explained. I don't know that such a procedure can either be justified or condemned altogether, any more than translation as a whole can be. Auden, for one, thought it the best possible way of going about it. I suspect it depends on the circumstances —who is doing the work, and their relation to each other and to the poetry they are translating. I have had my doubts about working this way, and have resolved several times not to do any more translation of this kind (as I have resolved not to translate any more at all) but I have succumbed repeatedly to particular material.

I should make it clear that the only languages from which I can translate directly are Romance languages, and that I am less familiar with Italian and Portuguese than with French and Spanish. All the translations from other sources, in this collection, were based on someone else's knowledge.

W. S. M

A NOTE ON THE LANGUAGES

QUECHUA *is a major language of the Andean plateaus. At one time it was a principle language of the Incan Empire.*

TZOTZIL *and* TZELTAL *are Mayan languages of the highlands of Chiapas in southern Mexico. Zinacantan and Tenejapa are villages;* TZOTZIL *is spoken in the former,* TZELTAL *in the latter.*

MALGACHE (*or* MALAGASY, *as it is anglicized*) *is the language of Madagascar.*

CONTENTS

Contents

Contents

I

FROM THE GREEK ANTHOLOGY

Julianus, Prefect of Egypt—5th century A.D.

Though you rule the dead, under the earth, who never smile,
    Persephone, welcome the shade of the gentle laughter,
Democritus. It was laughter alone that led
      your mother away from grief, when her heart was sore,
          after she lost you.

1971   *(Indicates date of translation)*

Epitaph for Cleonicus

Automedon   *dates unknown*

You who will die, watch over your life; don't set sail
    at the wrong season, for at best no man lives long.
Poor Cleonicus, so impatient to reach
    bright Thasos, trading out of hollow Syria,
trading, Cleonicus, sailing just as the Pleiades
    were setting, so that you and the Pleiades sank together.

1971

Gifts to a lady

Antiphilos   1st century A.D.

I've not much of my own, lady, mistress, but I
    believe that the man who's yours heart and soul stands
a full head above most men's riches.
    Accept this tunic, the soft pile of flowered purple,
this rose-red wool, this nard in a green glass
    for your dark hair. I want the first to enfold your body,
the wool to draw out the skill of your fingers,
    the scent to find its way through your hair.

1971

A quince preserved through the winter, given to a lady

Antiphilos   1st century A.D.

I'm a quince, saved over from last year, still fresh,
    my skin young, not spotted or wrinkled, downy as the
        new-born,
as though I were still among my leaves. Seldom
    does winter yield such gifts, but for you, my queen,
even the snows and frosts bear harvests like this.

1971

On the death of the ferryman, Glaucus

Antiphilos   1st century A.D.

Glaucus, pilot of the Nessus Strait, born
    on the coast of Thasos, skilled sea-plowman,
who moved the tiller unerringly even in his sleep,
    old beyond reckoning, a rag of a sailor's life,
even when death came would not leave his weathered deck.
    They set fire to the husk with him under it
so the old man might sail his own boat to Hades.

1971

Very dear though it was I have bought you
a little whatever-it-is for its sweet smell
since by the scent often I find the way
Wherever you are wherever I am
beyond all doubt I will be clear and certain
If you hide yourself from me I pardon you
Taking it always with you where you go
even if I were quite blind I would find you

1973

THE INFINITE

Leopardi   Italian   1798–1837

I always loved this hill by itself
and this line of bushes that hides
so much of the farthest horizon from sight.
But sitting looking out I imagine spaces
beyond this one, each without end,
and silences more than human, and a stillness
under it all, until my heart is drawn
to the edge of fear. And when the wind
rustles through the undergrowth near me
endlessly I compare its voice
with the infinite silence. I remember eternity
and the ages dead, and the present,
alive, and the sound of it. So in this
immensity my thinking drowns,
and sinking is sweet to me in this sea.

1971

THE MAN FROM UP-COUNTRY TALKING

João Cabral de Melo Neto   Portuguese   1920—

The man from up-country coats his talk:
the words come out of him like wrapped candy
(candy words, pills) in the icing
of a smooth intonation, sweetened.
While under the talk the core of stone
keeps hardening, the stone almond
from the rocky tree back where he comes from:
it can express itself only in stone.

That's why the man from up-country says little:
the stone words ulcerate the mouth
and it hurts to speak in the stone language;
those to whom it's native speak by main force.
Furthermore, that's why he speaks slowly:
he has to take up the words carefully,
he has to sweeten them with his tongue, candy them;
well, all this work takes time.

1969

TWO OF THE FESTIVALS
OF DEATH

João Cabral de Melo Neto   Portuguese   1920—

Solemn receptions given by death:
death, dressed for an unveiling;
and ambiguously: dressed like an orator
and like the statue that's to be unveiled.
In the coffin, half coffin half pedestal,
death unveils himself more than he dies;
and in duplicate: now he's his own statue,
now he's himself, alive, for the occasion.

Children's picnics given by death:
children's funerals in the northeast:
no one over thirteen admitted,
no adults allowed, even walking behind.
Party half outing half picnic,
in the open air, nice for a day when school's out;
the children who go play dolls
or else that's what they really are.

1969

THE DRAFTED VULTURE

João Cabral de Melo Neto   Portuguese   1920—

1.

When the droughts hit the backlands, they make
the vulture into a civil servant—free no more.
He doesn't try to escape. He's known for a long time
that they'd put his technique and his touch to use.
He says nothing of services rendered, of diplomas
which entitle him to better pay.
He serves the drought-dealers like an altar-boy,
with a greenhorn zeal, veteran though he is,
mercifully dispatching some who may not be dead,
when in private life he cares only for bona fide corpses.

2.

Though the vulture's a conscript, you can soon tell
from his demeanor that he's a real professional:
his self-conscious air, hunched and advisory,
his umbrella completeness, the clerical smoothness
with which he acts, even in a minor capacity—
an unquestioning liberal professional.

1969

INSTRUCTS HOW ALL THINGS
FORETELL DEATH

Francisco de Quevedo   Spanish   1580–1645

for Ines Kinnell

My country I saw its walls
that were strong at one time
but are going
weary of age his round

I went out to fields saw the sun
drinking streams
only thawed
and from the mount the crying herds
whose shadows stole
from the day its light

I went into my house
defaced
ruined old dwelling place
my staff more bent
also weaker

age had beat down my sword
and there was nowhere
to turn my eyes toward
but death also was coming there

1968

LOVE CONSTANT BEYOND DEATH

Francisco de Quevedo   Spanish   1580–1645

Last of the shadows may close my eyes
goodbye then white day
and with that my soul untie
its dear wishing

yet will not forsake
memory of this shore where it burned
but still burning swim
that cold water again
careless of the stern law

soul that kept God in prison
veins that to love led such fire
marrow that flamed in glory

not their heeding will leave
with their body
but being ash will feel
dust be dust in love

1968

This iron chain,
heavy as it is, seems
light to me, I don't feel it.
There's another chain made
of waves, lands, winds,
smiles, sighs,
that binds me I don't know where,
that enslaves me to that master
I don't know, that master . . .

1968

I can't see you but I know
you're right there on the other side
of a thin wall
of bricks and lime where
you'd hear if I called.
But I won't call.
I'll call you tomorrow
when not seeing you
makes me think you're still
there close beside me
and that all I need today
is the voice I withheld
yesterday.
Tomorrow when you're
there on the other side
of a thin wall of winds
skies, years.

1968

HER ABSENCE

Pedro Salinas   Spanish   1892–1951

You're not here. What I see of you,
a body, is a shadow, a trick.
Your soul has gone where you
yourself will be tomorrow.
Still this afternoon offers me
false hostages, aimless
smiles, idle gestures,
a love distracted.
You wanted to go and it took you
where you wanted to be,
far from here, where you
are saying to me,
"Here I am, with you, look."
And you point to your absence.

1968

GOODBYE

Pedro Salinas   Spanish   1892–1951

We're leaning
on the railing
over the water of goodbye.
It's neither muddy nor empty.
It has clouds, leaves in it, flights
in it
coming and going, and going
without a sound.

Numbers are floating there, letters,
loose, on top of it;
they don't add up to anything, don't
say anything.
Elysian figures, letters
in the garb of paradise,
assumption and holiday,
ready for another life.
You're much clearer in the water goodbye
than in your face.
You're much clearer in the water goodbye
than in my soul.
Now you'll never leave
here.
You'll live that way, outside
your face and my soul,
a third, made of you and me,
new,
cool daughter of goodbye.
Live:
see ourselves in goodbye.

1968

FURTHER QUESTION

Pedro Salinas   Spanish   1892–1951

Why do I ask where you are
if I'm not blind
and you're not absent?

If I see you
go and come,
you, your tall body
ending in a voice
as a flame ends in smoke
in the air, untouchable.

And I ask you, yes,
and I ask you
what you're made of
and whose you are
and you open your arms
and show me
the tall image of yourself
and say it's mine.

And I go on asking, forever.

1968

Not in marble palaces,
not in months, no, nor in numbers,
never treading the ground:
in frail worlds without weight
we have lived together.
Time was scarcely
reckoned in minutes:
one minute was a century,
a life, a love.
Roofs sheltered us.
Less than roofs, clouds.
Less than clouds: skies.
Still less: air, nothing.
Crossing
seas made of twenty tears,
ten of yours ten of mine,
we came to beads
of gold,
immaculate islands, deserted,
without flowers or flesh:
so small a lodging,
and of glass, for a love
able to reach, by itself,
the greatest longing,
and that asked no help
of ships or time.
Opening
enormous galleries
in the grains of sand,

we discovered the mines
of flames or of chance.
And all
hanging from that thread
that was held—by whom?
That's why our life doesn't seem
to have been lived.
Elusive as quicksilver,
it left neither wake
nor track. If you want
to remember it, don't look
in footsteps or memory,
where people always look.
Don't look in the soul,
in the shadows, in the lips.
Look carefully in the palm
of the hand: empty.

1968

POETRY IS A HEAVENLY CRIME

Vicente Huidobro   Spanish   1893–1948

I am absent but deep in this absence
There is the waiting for myself
And this waiting is another form of presence
The waiting for my return
I am in other objects
I am away travelling giving a little of my life
To some trees and some stones
That have been waiting for me many years

They got tired of waiting for me and sat down

I'm not here and I'm here
I'm absent and I'm present in a state of waiting
They wanted my language so they could express themselves
And I wanted theirs to express them
This is the ambiguity, the horrible ambiguity

Tormented wretched
I'm moving inward on these soles
I'm leaving my clothes behind
My flesh is falling away on all sides
And my skeleton's putting on bark

I'm turning into a tree How often I've turned into other
      things . . .
It's painful and full of tenderness

I could cry out but it would scare off the transubstantiation
Must keep silence Wait in silence

1970

20

MY WHOLE LIFE

Jorge Luis Borges   Spanish   1899—

Here once again the memorable lips, unique and like yours.
I am this groping intensity that is a soul.
I have got near to happiness and have stood in the shadow of
  suffering.
I have crossed the sea.
I have known many lands; I have seen one woman and two
  or three men.
I have loved a girl who was fair and proud, with a Spanish
  quietness.
I have seen the city's edge, an endless sprawl where the sun
  goes down tirelessly, over and over.
I have relished many words.
I believe deeply that this is all and that I will neither see nor
  accomplish new things.
I believe that my days and my nights, in their poverty and
  their riches, are the equal of God's and of all men's.

1968

TO A MINOR POET OF THE
GREEK ANTHOLOGY

Jorge Luis Borges   Spanish   1899—

Where now is the memory
of the days that were yours on earth, and wove
joy with sorrow, and made a universe that was your own?

The river of years has lost them
from its numbered current; you are a word in an index.

To others the gods gave glory that has no end:
inscriptions, names on coins, monuments, conscientious
     historians;
all that we know of you, eclipsed friend,
is that you heard the nightingale one evening.

Among the asphodels of the Shadow, your shade, in its
     vanity,
must consider the gods ungenerous.

But the days are a web of small troubles
and is there a greater blessing
than to be the ash of which oblivion is made?

Above other heads the gods kindled
the inexorable light of glory, which peers into the secret parts
     and discovers each separate fault;
glory, that at last shrivels the rose it reveres;
they were more considerate with you, brother.

In the rapt evening that will never be night
you listen without end to Theocritus' nightingale.

1968

THE POET TELLS OF HIS FAME

Jorge Luis Borges   Spanish   1899—

The rim of the sky is the measure of my glory,
The libraries of the East argue over my verses,
The rulers seek me out to fill my mouth with gold,
The angels already know my last couplet by heart.
The tools of my art are humiliation and anguish.
Oh if only I had been born dead!

From the Divan of Abulcasim El Hadrami (12th Century)

1968

A MAN

Nicanor Parra   Spanish   1914—

A man's mother is very sick
He goes out to find a doctor
He's crying
In the street he sees his wife in the company of another man
They're holding hands
He follows them a short distance
From tree to tree
He's crying
Now he meets a friend from his youth
It's years since we've seen each other!
They go on to a bar
They talk, laugh
The man goes out to the patio for a piss
He sees a young girl
It's night
She's washing dishes
The man goes over to her
He takes her by the waist
They waltz
They go out into the street together
They laugh
There's an accident
The girl's lost consciousness
The man goes to telephone
He's crying
He comes to a house with lights on
He asks for a telephone
Somebody knows him
Hey stay and have something to eat
No

Where's the telephone
Have something to eat, hey eat something
Then go
He sits down to eat
He drinks like a condemned man
He laughs
They get him to recite something
He recites it
He ends up sleeping under a desk

1970

SONG OF THE FOREIGNER

Nicanor Parra   Spanish   1914—

Travelling man
come into this room
coming out of bathroom
sit on precious chair
in front of birror
oped his fly

The cloud cover the sun
I cover the cloud with left hand
I spit blood
So bad danger the sky send

Me going in cemetery
me cry very much for dead one used to married to
me put urn in nitz
not let nobody touch him
I kiss him urn—I hug him urn—I everything

I buy him most prettiest urn
with precious crucifix
I put him myself in coffin
I cry—I laugh because with great suffering
I customer and sell you little comb cheap

1970

PROPOSALS

Nicanor Parra   Spanish   1914—

I'm sad I've got nothing to eat
nobody cares about me
there shouldn't be any beggars
I've been saying the same thing for years

I propose that instead of butterflies
lobsters should move in the gardens
—I think that would be a lot better—
can you imagine a world without beggars?

I propose that we all turn catholic
or communist or whatever you like
it's only a difference of words
I propose that we purify the water

with the authority given me by my beggar's stick
I propose that the pope grow a moustache

I'm starting to feel faint with hunger
I propose that they give me a sandwich
and to end the monotony I propose
that the sun should rise in the west

1970

I Jehovah Decree

that they get it over with once and for all
I'm giving the solar system the slip

everything back into the womb
I'm saying it's over finished and done with

nobody's escaping
everything over with in one stroke
why beat around the bush

great thing the Vietnam War
great thing the Prostate Operation
I Jehovah decree old age

you people make me laugh
you people give me the creeps
only a born moron
could get down on his knees and worship a statue

frankly I don't know what to tell you
we're on the brink of the Third World War
and nobody seems to have noticed

if you destroy the world
do you think I'm going to create it over again?

1970

EVERYTHING USED TO LOOK GOOD TO ME

Nicanor Parra   Spanish   1914—

Now everything looks bad to me

an old telephone with a little bell
was enough to make me the happiest creature alive
an arm chair—almost anything

Sunday mornings
I'd go to the flea market
and come back with a wall clock
—anyway with the case—
or with a pensioned off victrola
to my shack at La Reina
where Chamaco was waiting for me
and the lady who used to be his mother
in those days

those were happy days
or at least nights without pain

1970

ELEGY

Juan José Arreola   Spanish   1918—

Those vague scars that can be seen there among the plowed fields are the ruins of the camp of Nobilior. Farther on rise the military positions of Castillejo, Renieblas, and Peña Redona . . .

Nothing is left of the distant city except one hill heavy with silence. And next to it, running beside it, that ruin of a river. The little stream Merdancho hums its ballad refrain, and resounds with epic greatness only in the sudden flash-floods of June.

This tranquil plain witnessed the succession of incompetent generals. Nobilior, Lepidus, Furius Filus, Caius Hostilius Mancinus . . . And among them the poet Lucilius, who sauntered there with the airs of an conqueror, and returned to Rome ill-used and beaten, his sword and his lyre both dragging, and his sharp tongue blunted.

Legions upon legions were shattered against those invincible walls. Thousands of soldiers went down under the arrows, despair, the winter. Until one day the enraged Scipio loomed up on the horizon like an avenging wave and seized in his unyielding hands the tough neck of Numancia, month after month without letting go.

1969

THE CAVE

Juan José Arreola   Spanish   1918—

Nothing but horror, pure and empty. That is the cave of Tribenciano. A stone void in the bowels of the earth. A cavity, long and rounded like an egg. Two hundred meters long, eighty wide. A dome in every direction, of marbled smooth stone.

There are seventy steps going down to the cave, arranged in flights of different lengths, along a natural fissure that opens like an ordinary crack in the ground. What does one go down to? At one time it was to die. There are bones on the cave floor, and quantities of bone dust. No one knows whether the nameless victims went down of their own free will or were sent there by some special order. And whose?

Some students of the cave are convinced that it is not the abode of any cruel mystery. They say that it all has to do with an ancient cemetery, perhaps Etruscan, perhaps Ligurian. But no one can remain in that cavern for more than five minutes: he runs the risk of completely losing his mind.

Men of science prefer to explain the fainting that overcomes those who venture inside by saying that underground gas leaks seep into the cave. But no one knows what kind of gas it might be or where it comes from. It may be that what seizes a man there is the horror of pure space: nothing, in its concave muteness.

No more is known about the cave of Tribenciano. Thousands of cubic meters of nothing in its round pot. Nothing, in a rind of stone. Holding death dust.

1969

TELEMACHUS

Juan José Arreola   Spanish   1918—

Wherever there's a fight I'll be on the side that falls. Now it's heroes or thugs.

I'm tied by the neck to the slave concept carved on the oldest standing stones. I'm the dying warrior under Asurbanipal's chariot, and the calcined bone in the ovens of Dachau.

Hector and Menelaus, France and Germany, and the two drunks who push in each other's faces in the bar wear me out with their disputes. Wherever I turn my eyes the landscape of the world is hidden by an enormous Veronica's Veil showing the face of the Despised Good.

I the observer of force see which of the combatants starts the fight, and I want to be on no one's side. Because I also am two: the one who strikes and the one who received the blows.

Man against man. Any bets?

Ladies and gentlemen, there is no salvation. The game is being lost within ourselves. At this moment the Devil's playing with the white pieces.

1969

DEER

Juan José Arreola   Spanish   1918—

Outside space and time the deer wander, at once swift and languid, and no one knows whether their true place is in immobility or in movement; they combine the two in such a way that we are forced to place them in eternity.

Inert or dynamic, they keep changing the natural horizon, and they perfect our ideas of time, space, and the laws of moving bodies. Made expressly to solve the ancient paradox, they are at once Achilles and the tortoise, the bow and the arrow. They run without ever overtaking. They stop and something remains always outside them, galloping.

The deer cannot stand still, but moves forward like an apparition, whether it be among real trees or out of a grove in a legend: Saint Hubert's Stag bearing a cross between his antlers, or the doe that gives suck to Genevieve de Brabant. Wherever they are encountered, the male and the female comprise the same fabulous pair.

Quarry without peer, all of us mean to take it, even if only with the eyes. And if Juan de Yepes tells us that what he pursued, when hunting, was so high, so high—he is not referring to the earthly dove, but to the deer: profound, unattainable, and in flight.

1969

Sometimes my hands wake me up.
They're making or taking apart something without me
while I'm asleep,
something terribly human,
concrete like the back or pocket of a man.

I hear them from inside my sleep,
working out there,
but when I open my eyes they're still.
Just the same
I've thought that maybe I'm a man
because of what they do
with their gestures and not mine,
with their God and not mine,
with their death, if they die too.

I don't know how to make a man.
Maybe my hands make one while I'm asleep
and when it's finished
they wake me up altogether
and show it to me.

1971

A man spells out his tiredness.
All at once as he spells
he meets some strange capital letters,
unexpectedly alone,
unexpectedly tall.
They weigh more on the tongue.
They weigh more but they get away
faster and hardly
can they be spoken.
His heart crowds into the roads
where death is exploding.
And he meets, as he goes on spelling,
bigger and bigger capital letters.
And a great fear chokes him
of finding a word
written all in capitals
and not being able to pronounce it.

1971

There will come a day
when we won't need to push on the panes for them to fall,
nor hammer the nails for them to hold,
nor walk on the stones to keep them quiet,
nor drink the faces of women for them to smile.

It will be the beginning of the great union.
Even God will learn how to talk,
and the air and the light
will enter their cave of shy eternities.

Then there'll be no more difference between your eyes and
        your belly,
nor between my words and my mouth.
The stones will be like your breasts
and I will make my verses with my hands
so that nobody can be mistaken.

1971

Life draws a tree
and death draws another one.
Life draws a nest
and death copies it.
Life draws a bird
to live in the nest
and right away death
draws another bird.

A hand that draws nothing
wanders among the drawings
and at times moves one of them.
For example:
a bird of life
occupies death's nest
on the tree that life drew.

Other times
the hand that draws nothing
blots out one drawing of the series.
For example:
the tree of death
holds the nest of death,
but there's no bird in it.

And other times
the hand that draws nothing
itself changes
into an extra image

in the shape of a bird,
in the shape of a tree,
in the shape of a nest.
And then, only then,
nothing's missing and nothing's left over.
For example:
two birds
occupy life's nest
in death's tree.

Or life's tree
holds two nests
with only one bird in them.

Or a single bird
lives in the one nest
on the tree of life
and the tree of death.

1970

I'm awake.
I'm asleep.
I'm dreaming that I'm awake.
I'm dreaming that I'm asleep.
I'm dreaming that I'm dreaming.

I'm dreaming that I'm dreaming
that I'm awake.
I'm dreaming that I'm dreaming
that I'm asleep.
I'm dreaming that I'm dreaming
that I'm dreaming.

I'm awake.

1971

If we knew the point
where something is going to break,
where the thread of kisses will be cut,
where a look will no longer meet another,
where the heart will leap toward another place,
we could put another point on that point
or at least go with it to its breaking.

If we knew the point
where something is going to melt into something,
where the desert will meet the rain,
where the embrace will touch life itself,
where my death will come closer to yours,
we could unwind that point like a streamer,
or at least sing it till we died.

If we knew the point
where something will always be something,
where the bone will not forget the flesh,
where the fountain is mother to another fountain,
where the past will never be past,
we could retain that point and erase all the others,
or at least keep it in a safer place.

(To Laura)

1971

FROM DIARIO SEMANARIO

Jaime Sabines   Spanish   1925—

At midnight, exactly at the end of August, I think sadly of the leaves falling incessantly from the calendars. I feel that I am the tree of the calendars.

Every day, my child, going away forever, leaves me asking myself, "If someone who loses a parent is an orphan, if someone who loses a wife is a widower, what is the name for someone who loses a child? What do you call someone who loses time? And if I myself am time, what can I call myself, if I lose myself?"

Day and night, not Monday or Tuesday, not August or September, day and night are the only measure of our duration. To exist is to continue—to open your eyes and close them.

At these hours, each night, forever, I am he who has lost the day. (Even though I feel, in the heart of these hours, the dawn, like the fruit in the branches of the peach tree, climbing.)

1971

I HAVE EYES TO SEE . . .

Jaime Sabines   Spanish   1925—

I have eyes to see in this night
something of what I am, my hearing is hearing.
I am in this room, so are my dreams.

Back of each shadow there's something of mine.
There's one sitting on each chair, dark,
and at my feet, in bed, they're seeing me.
I believe they're like me, they bear my name
and they emerge from things, like mirrors.

It's already a long time
since we last assembled.
Now I give them lodging
humbly,
I give them my body.

I come together again at night, I open my eyes,
I wet them with this darkness full of dream.
Only my heart on top of the sheet
Still beating.

1971

FROM THE BODIES

Jaime Sabines   Spanish   1925—

From the blue and black bodies
that walk at times through my soul
come voices and signs that someone interprets.
It's dark as the sun
this desire. Mysterious and grave
as an ant dragging away the wing of a butterfly
or as the yes that we say when things ask us
—do you want to live?

1971

I'M OUT TO FIND A MAN

Jaime Sabines   Spanish   1925—

I'm out to find a man who looks like me
to give him my name and my wife and my son,
my books and my debts.
I'm going looking for someone to give him my soul,
my fate, my death.

With what pleasure I'd do it,
with what tenderness I'd leave myself in his hands!

1971

YOU HAVE WHAT I LOOK FOR

Jaime Sabines   Spanish   1925—

You have what I look for, what I long for, what I love,
you have it.
The fist of my heat is beating, calling.
I thank the stories for you,
I thank your mother and your father
and death who has not seen you.
I thank the air for you.
You are elegant as wheat,
delicate as the outline of your body.
I have never loved a slender woman
but you have made my hands fall in love,
you moored my desire,
you caught my eyes like two fish.
And for this I am at your door, waiting.

1975

THE CONCEITED

Roque Dalton Spanish 1935—

I'd be wonderful at being dead.

Then my vices would shine like ancient jewels
with those delicious colors of poison.

There'd be flowers of every scent on my tomb
and the adolescents would imitate my expressions of joy,
my occult words of anguish.

Maybe somebody'd say I was loyal and good.
But you'd be the only one who'd remember
the way I looked into eyes.

1971

PILGRIM SONGS

Anonymous   Russian   19th century

I.

Come children of the same family
listen to the word
    of the Lord
what it says about our life

the life of someone on earth
    is like the grass growing in the fields
the mind in each person
    blossoms like the flowers

and to the last evening
    a body is happy
but in the morning
    it lies in its grave
the quick legs
    out from under it
the white hands fallen

there was not even time
to press the hands
to the racing heart

oh you there what good is it
for them to wash your dead body
when you never bathed it in tears
    before the Lord

oh you there what good is it
wrapping you in vestments
when you never wrapped yourself
    in vestments of the spirit

oh you there what good is it
lighting candles over you
when you kept no lamp burning
    in your heart
      before the Lord

oh you there what good is it
performing a service over you
when you never performed
    what God commanded

oh you there what good is it
to go with your corpse
    to God's church
when you had no spiritual father
    and never repented your sins

all your glory has gone now
all you possessed stayed here

the soul has said goodbye
    to its white body
and the mind is parting from its head
    from that precious one

and for all times
have mercy on us

2.

Our life on earth
    is like the grass growing
and the mind in us
    is like the opened flowers

in the evening
    a body is happy
by morning that same one
    lies in the grave
bright eyes clouded
    quick legs gone from under

if you want to escape
    eternal pain
take a candle of pure gold
    and its adornments
enter into joy
    with the bridegroom
and reign forever

oh you there go up
onto the mountain of Zion
and listen a while
        oh you
to the loud trumpet sound
the trumpet sounding the truth
the herald of heaven

1977   *translated with* ALLA BURAGO

Beyond the mountains beyond the forests
beyond the dust of the roads
beyond the grave mounds
under other skies you flower

Whiteness will spread on the mountain
but spring will come back to the valley
and I will recall with an older sadness
my past as though it were yesterday

In the grief of my dreams I will know you
and I will seize in my palms
your gentle hand that has borne miracles
and repeat the distance in your name

30 September 1915

1968

LENINGRAD

Osip Mandelstam   Russian   1891—1938

I've come back to my city. These are my own old tears,
my own little veins, the swollen glands of my childhood.

So you're back. Open wide. Swallow
the fish-oil from the river lamps of Leningrad.

Open your eyes. Do you know this December day,
the egg-yolk with the deadly tar beaten into it?

Petersburg! I don't want to die yet!
You know my telephone numbers.

Petersburg! I've still got the addresses:
I can look up dead voices.

I live on back stairs, and the bell,
torn out nerves and all, jangles in my temples.

And I wait till morning for guests that I love,
and rattle the door in its chains.

Leningrad. December 1930

1972   translated with CLARENCE BROWN

Your thin shoulders are for turning red under whips,
turning red under whips, and flaming in the raw cold.

Your child's fingers are for lifting flatirons,
for lifting flatirons, and for knotting cords.

Your tender soles are for walking on broken glass,
walking on broken glass, across bloody sand.

And I'm for burning like a black candle lit for you,
for burning like a black candle that dare not pray.

1934

1972   translated with CLARENCE BROWN

Now I'm dead in the grave with my lips moving
and every schoolboy repeating the words by heart.

The earth is rounder in Red Square than anywhere,
all one side of a hardened will.

The earth in Red Square is rounder than anywhere.
No one would think it was so light of heart

bending back all the way down to the rice growing
on the last day of the last slave on the globe.

Voronezh. May 1935

1972   translated with CLARENCE BROWN

How dark it gets along the Kama.
The cities kneel by the river on oaken knees.

Draped in cobwebs, beard with beard,
black firs and their reflections run back into their childhood.

The water leaned into fifty-two pairs of oars,
pushed them upstream, downstream, to Kazan and Cherdyn.

There I floated with a curtain across the window,
a curtain across the window, and the flame inside was my head.

And my wife was with me there five nights without sleeping,
five nights awake keeping an eye on the guards.

Voronezh. May 1935

1972   translated with CLARENCE BROWN

Today is all beak and no feathers
and it's staying that way. Why?
And a gate by the sea gazes at me
out of anchors and fogs.

Quietly, quietly warships are gliding
through faded water,
and in canals gaunt as pencils
under the ice the leads go on blackening.

Voronezh. 9–28 December 1936

1972   translated with CLARENCE BROWN

Mounds of human heads are wandering into the distance.
I dwindle among them. Nobody sees me. But in books
much loved, and in children's games I shall rise
from the dead to say the sun is shining.

1936–1937?

1972   translated with CLARENCE BROWN

THE LAST SUPPER

Osip Mandelstam   Russian   1891—1938

The heaven of the supper fell in love with the wall.
It filled it with cracks. It fills them with light.
It fell into the wall. It shines out there
in the form of thirteen heads.

And that's my night sky, before me,
and I'm the child standing under it,
my back getting cold, an ache in my eyes,
and the wall-battering heaven battering me.

At every blow of the battering ram
stars without eyes rain down,
new wounds in the last supper,
the unfinished mist on the wall.

Voronezh. 9 March 1937

1972   translated with CLARENCE BROWN

Today everything
is earnest and hushed.
As at the death of a queen
when the radio changes from light music
to Mozart or Bach.
I don't know why.
Since she isn't listening.
I can almost see
how people leave
each other, how silence
works in the fading fabrics
and how the solitary
gray wasp gropes its way
into its death sleep
in the wound of the dry mountain tree.

1975   translated with GUNNAR HARDING

Maybe this road
leads nowhere but someone
is coming from there

1976   translated with GUNNAR HARDING

ON NELLY SACHS

Lars Noren   Swedish   1944—

Toward the end
her eyes grew
younger and younger
as though they had been watching
what can be understood but not said
They weighed almost nothing
and must have been like the rabbit's
breath in winter air after it has been shot

1976   translated with GUNNAR HARDING

Lars Noren   Swedish   1944—

When I travel back to my
own birth and existence
there is no mother there
and I have to give birth to her

1976   translated with GUNNAR HARDING

58

II

Whatever place
I come on trouble
my death will not be there

I shall pass through

though there may be many arrows
I shall reach
where I am going

as the heart of a man should be
mine is

1969

If all of me is still there
    when spring comes
    I'll make a hundred poles

    and put something on top
    sun

    for you
    you

right there I'll make a small sweat lodge
    it's cold
    I'll sprinkle charcoal

    at the end of it
    my death

    sun
    it will all be for you

I want to be still there
    that's why I'll do it

    thank you

I want to be alive

If my people multiply
    I'll make it for you

I'm saying
    may no one be sick

    so I make it

    so

1970

If there is someone above
who knows what happens

You

today I have trouble
give me something to make it
not so

if there is someone inside the earth
who knows what happens

I have trouble today
give me something
to make it not so

whatever makes these things
now just as I am
I have enough

give me just for me
my death

I have enough sadness

1969

Crow   from Robert Lowie's "Crow Texts"

Your way
   is turning bad

   and nobody but you
   is there

1970

Crow   from Robert Lowie's "Crow Texts"

Child listen
   I am singing

   with my ear on the ground

   and we love you

1970

Crow from Robert Lowie's "Crow Texts"

I am climbing
  everywhere is

coming up

1970

Crow from Robert Lowie's "Crow Texts"

I am making
  a wind come here

it's coming

1970

Crow from Robert Lowie's "Crow Texts"

Heaven
Earth
  always there

the old fill up
  with trouble

don't be afraid

1970

PRAYER

Anonymous   Quechua   adapted from Spanish

Oh you

from whom it came
   comes
   you
lord of what is

whether you're
   a man
whether you're
   a woman
   lord
of what's born

whatever you are
lord of the sight beyond

where are you

you above at this moment
you below at this moment

presence
throne sceptre
   shining around them

hear
me

maybe the sky is your floor
maybe the sea is your roof
    maker of above and below

as we are you made us
lord above lords

my eyes are weak
with longing to see you
    only with longing
to know you

make it be
    that I see you
make it be
    that I know you
make it be
  that I hold you in my thought
make it be
    that you are clear in my mind

look at me
for you know me

sun and moon
day and night
spring and winter
you set them in order
    you

    from whom it came
    comes
all of them run
    the course you marked out for them
all of them reach

the goal you set for them
wherever you wanted it

you bearing
the king's sceptre

hear me
choose me

do not let me grow tired
do not let me die

1970

PRAYER

Anonymous   Quechua   adapted from Spanish

Come closer truth from above us
truth from below us

who made the form of the world

　　you
　　who let it all exist

　　who alone made humans

ten times with eyes full of darkness
　　I must worship you

　　saying Brightness

　　stretched out before you

look at me
　　lord
　　notice me

　　and your rivers your waterfalls
　　your birds

　　give me your
　　life
　　all you can

　　help me to call
　　with your voices

even now we taste
    the joy of your will
    and we remember it all
    we are happy

even so we are filled
    as we go away
    as we go

1970

Where are you where are you going
they say
and we still have to go on

sun and moon go past
   and go past
   six months to get from Cuzco to Quito

at the foot of Tayo we'll rest

fear nothing
lord Inca fear nothing
we're going with you we'll get there together

1970

I'm bringing up a fly
    with golden wings
    bringing up a fly
    with eyes burning

it carries death
    in its eyes of fire
carries death
    in its golden hair
    in its gorgeous wings

in a green bottle
    I'm bringing it up

        nobody knows
        if it drinks

        nobody knows
        if it eats

at night it goes wandering
    like a star

        wounding to death
        with red rays
        from its eyes of fire

it carries love
    in its eyes of fire
    flashes in the night

its blood
the love it bears in its breast

insect of night
fly bearing death

in a green bottle
I'm bringing it up
I love it
that much

but nobody
no
nobody knows

if I give it to drink
nobody knows if I feed it

1970

When you find you're alone on the island in the river
your father won't be there
to call you
    aloo
    my daughter
your mother won't be able
to reach you
    aloo
    my daughter

only the royal duck will stay near you
with the rain in its eyes
with tears of blood
    with the rain in its eyes
    tears of blood

and even the royal duck will leave you
when the waves of the river
    boil
when the waves
    race on the river

but then I'll go and stay near you
singing
    I'll steal her young heart
    on the island

    her young heart
    in the storm

1970

It's today I'm supposed
    to go away
I won't
    I'll go
    tomorrow

you'll see me go
    playing a flute
made from a bone of a fly

    carrying a flag
made from a spider's web

    beating an ant's egg
drum

with a humming-bird's nest for a hat
    with my head
    in a humming-bird's nest

1970

PRAYER TO THE CORN
IN THE FIELD

Tzeltal (Tenejapa)

Sacred food
sacred bones

don't go to another house
don't go at all

come straight in to us
stay right on the trail

to the house
to your bed

don't go crying like an orphan
to another plant

another stone
another cave

kernels that fall out of you
that I didn't find to pick up

if there are those of you
who were taken from your places

by the mountain lion
by the squirrel

by the coyote
by the fox

by the pig
by the thief

come back along the trail
to our house

the whole time
to our place

don't get smaller
going away

from our feet
from our hands

1971 from a literal version by KATHERINE B. BRANSTETTER
informant Am Perez Mesa

THE FLOOD

Tzotzil (Zinacantan)

There were still three suns in the sky
And the first people were dwarfs
And the flood came.

And they died
Some died.

And they shut themselves up in coffins
Some.
And they climbed trees
Some.
They broke the stones of fruit with their teeth.
Their meals were acorns
When the world was flooded
At one time.

Well they changed.
Their tails sprouted.
And hair grew on them.
Then they were monkeys.

Well that is how the world ended
At one time.

Then came a change of people.
It was us.

The dwarfs are below.
But often they talk with the gods.
They are tired of it underground.

The sun burns too much there.
They are tired of having nothing but mud to wear.
Mud hats to keep the sun off.

They want to come up here.

So now this world can't last long.

1971 from a version by ROBERT LAUGHLIN
informant Domingo de la Torre P.

BELLY-ACHE

Tzotzil (Zinacantan)

They were in bed together, the woman had a husband, the woman's husband came, spoke with his sister-in-law, talked with her, went to bed with her, didn't know whether there was another, her husband came, his house was closed, he went in to find them, he opened the door, her husband, they are one on top of the other, one on top of his sister-in-law, he wants to kill them, the husband, they changed into birds, they flew away, they went out of the house, they went away until they were on the mountain. One said, "Belly-ache." The other answered, "My sister-in-law, belly-ache." They fly to the mountain. Both of them are crying there now on the mountain.

1971   from a Spanish literal version of ROBERT LAUGHLIN'S *informant S.A.*

STORY OF THE LAZY MAN
AND THE ANTS

Tzeltal (Tenejapa)

A man was very lazy at working.
A man feels he will never be finished working.
A man slept at his work.
A man didn't work much every day.
A man only felt like working a little bit every day.
Every day a man sleeps at his work.
When his work grabs him he scratches his head a lot.
Every day a man is just yawning at his work.
There is the sun.
Went to see the lazy man.
When the sun gets to the lazy man
He finds him sleeping at his work.
The lazy man is crying through his nose in his sleep. He is
    snoring.
The sun says, "What a lazy man at his work! What a lot he
    sleeps!"
The sun grabbed dust in his hand.
Three times.
The sun threw three handfuls of dust
Where the lazy man was sleeping.
The sun made the dust turn into ants.
Then the dust turned into ants.
The ants of earth fell onto the lazy man
Where he was sleeping.
The lazy man opened his eyes
Because of the ants.
The ants bit him and the bites hurt very much.
The lazy man lost his sleep

Because of the ants.
The lazy man's laziness all went out of him
Because of the ants biting him.
Every day a man does not sleep at his work.
In fact there are many ants at his work.
Long ago the sun turned dust into ants
Because of a lazy man.
Now on earth there are many ants
Because of lazy men.

1971 from a literal version by KATHERINE B. BRANSTETTER
informant Santiago Mendes Zapata

STORY OF THE EATERS

Tzeltal (Tenejapa)

The eaters saddened every heart in Tenejapa.
The eaters couldn't be seen.
The eaters had powers that could murder the souls of people.
The eaters he eats the souls of grown people and children.
The eaters had great powers they could eat the souls of the
    dead.
The eaters went walking every night to houses because he is
    looking for someone who is open to sickness.
Those who pray and burn candles to God himself
So the eaters won't eat them.
Whoever does not burn candles to God himself
Many eaters come to his house with diseases.
The eaters takes souls and locks them up in the low city.
The eaters he gives people vomiting, diarrhoea and headache.
When the eaters locks up souls in the low city
Prayers set them free.
They make prayers for the souls that are locked up.
They pray they burn thirteen candles
Thirteen balls of incense
Five liters of cane alcohol
And one jug of cane wine
And a chicken
And a pack of cigarettes
And four gourds of our tobacco.
Every night the eaters want people. They go to dogs.
If a dog is crying at night like an orphan
The eaters are counting its hairs for it.
The eaters count the dog's hairs when they want people for
    eating.
If it is not time for the dog's master to die

The dog tells the roosters
It's not time for his master to die.
The dog tells the roosters if the eaters come.
"Now you crow," the dog says, "because of my master."
The roosters are always ready
When the eater comes to the dog at night.
If the eater comes to the dog to count the dog's hairs
He stops half way for a rest counting the dog's hairs.
Then the dog cries like an orphan.
Then when the dog cries like an orphan all the roosters crow.
"Already the place is light.
Let's go now, the roosters are crowing,"
The eater says.
Thus no disease comes to the owners of the houses in Tenejapa.
In fact the dogs and the roosters protect it carefully from eaters.

1971   from a literal version by KATHERINE B. BRANSTETTER
informant Santiago Mendes Zapata

STORY OF THE ANTS AND GRASSHOPPERS

Tzeltal (Tenejapa)

Ants work very much every day none sleep
    in fact they use the daytime
at night they sleep they rest their hearts
    because of their work in the days
when in its time in its season the rain comes
    very much food the ants have gathered
    working in the clear weather
the ants feel no sadness because of the rains
    they feel no hunger with all that food
when the ants went to work in the cloudless season
    the grasshoppers laughed a lot and made fun of them
why ever should we go to work in fact
    in the clear weather they said
    the grasshoppers making fun of the ants
the grasshoppers did no work in the cornfields every day
    the grasshoppers sleep in the fields
in the nights the grasshoppers have parties
    with their music
all they know how to do at night is have parties with their
                              music
    no work to speak of
the grasshoppers make fun of the ants a lot
    for only working in the cornfields
it came the time of hunger the rainy season for them
    the grasshoppers
none the food of the grasshoppers in the time of the rainy
                          season in fact
    none their work in the clear weather
the grasshoppers suffered with hunger

the grasshoppers came to the ants' houses
won't you lend us some food because we ourselves are dying
of hunger
the grasshoppers said
there is this suffering of yours because there was no work you
did
in the cloudless weather in fact
in the daytime you slept in the night you had parties the
ants said
it is better to work in the clear weather than to be lazy and
walk around
and sleep and have parties in the fields
the ants said to the grasshoppers scolding them
we on the other hand did not sleep in the daytime the ants said
the ants laughed because the grasshoppers
were suffering from hunger
the grasshoppers were ashamed because the ants had uncovered
their shame
the grasshoppers began to steal because they were hungry
in the time long ago there were created
the grasshoppers the creatures who do not work in
cornfields
in the time long ago there were created the ants
who work hard in cornfields

1976 from a literal version by KATHERINE B. BRANSTETTER
informant Santiago Mendes Zapata

THE DREAM

Eskimo

Last night you were in a dream
I dreamed you
walking on the shore
over the little stones
and I was walking with you
last night when I dreamed about you
I dreamed I followed you
I thought I was awake
I wanted you
as though you were a young seal
you were what I wanted
as a young seal
in the eyes of a hunter
before it dives because it's being followed
you were what I wanted
that's how
I wanted you
in my dream about you

1969   from a French version by PAUL-ÉMILE VICTOR

SONG OF THE OLD WOMAN

Eskimo

A lot of heads around me
a lot of ears around me
a lot of eyes around me
will those ears hear me much longer
will those eyes see me much longer
when those ears don't hear me any more
when those eyes don't look at mine any more
I won't eat liver with blubber any more
then those eyes won't see me any more
and this hair will have disappeared from my head

1969 from a French version by PAUL-ÉMILE VICTOR

Eskimo

My song was ready
it was in my mouth
it was all ready
my song
but I gave up the hunt
because the sea got rough
the cold North wind blew
and I saw heavy fogs getting up
along the mountain I saw them running
I saw them getting up
the cold wet fogs out of the north sky

1969 from a French version by PAUL-ÉMILE VICTOR

Bear in mind
regrets
Andriamatoa

they aren't the man
who puts his head in the door
and you say
Come in

they aren't the man sitting there
and you say
Let me get by

they don't give you
any warning at all
just make fun of you afterwards

we can't drive them ahead of us
like sheep

they follow us
like dogs

they bounce up
behind
like sheep's tails

1970 from Les Hain-Tenys by JEAN PAULHAN

Now you're ripe for me
and I'm hungry for you

I want to peel you

even if the butterfly brushes you
the black butterfly
death

I won't leave you

he who dies for someone he loves
is a little alligator
whom his mother swallows

and he finds himself back again
in the belly he knows so well

1970   from Les Hain-Tenys by JEAN PAULHAN

MALAYAN FIGURES

Anonymous   Malay

Slow splashing splashing
wakes me
and I cling to the wet pillow

Stepping on a long thorn
to me the sight of her hair

I would die
of your fingers
if I could be buried in your palm

If you go upriver pick me a flower
if you die before me wait
just beyond the grave

Daybreak with clouds flying and one star
like a knife in the hill
if I could find her I would see nothing else

Unless she is the one
sail on to death
like an empty ship

The fish line goes out
and out
but one end is in my hand

Let us row over to the fort crusted with sea shells
even priests sin in spite of their learning
and what do we know

You knew what I was like
and you started it

The lime tree bends to the still water
how sweet your voice is
when you are thinking of another

If you know a song
sing it

Setting out for the island
forget all your clothes
but not me

1970

KOREAN FIGURES

Anonymous   Korean

Even with your aunt
bargain

You give the child
you don't like
one extra

Wash a bean
that's how polished
he seems

For every beggar
a day comes
bringing a guest

Blind
blames the ditch

Can't see
steal your own things

Blind horse
follows
bells

All dressed up
walking in the dark

I eat the cucumber
my way

Hunchback
is good to
his parents

Even on dog turds
the dew falls

Chased a chicken
stands looking up

A dog with
two back doors

Man with ten vices
sneers at the man with one

Each finger
can suffer

Needle thief
dreams
of spears

Quiet
like a house where the witch
has just stopped dancing

Sparrow shouts
in the teeth of death

A gentleman
would rather drown
than swim dogpaddle

Dress sword
and no pants

Gone like an egg in a river

Nobody notices hunger
but they never miss dirt

Every grave
holds a reason

1968

JAPANESE FIGURES

Anonymous   Japanese

Autumn rides down
on one leaf

Autumn
the deer's
own color

The world turns
through partings

Star
watching
the day break

Sudden
like a spear from a window

Feet of the lantern bearer
move in the dark

Better than the holiday
is the day before

Departs once
is forgotten day
after day

Spits straight up
learns something

When he talks
it clouds the tea

Summer rain
so hard
parted the horse's mane

Blind man
calling his
lost staff

Sparrows a hundred years old
still dance
the sparrow dance

Just got it
in time to lose it

If he flatters you
watch him

Autumn
glass sky
horses fattening

Bird flies up
where your foot was going

Wake up
as much as you can

Nobody bothers
the bad boys

Too big
to be bright all through

Keeps counting up
the dead child's
age

Death
collects all the tongues

One god goes
but another comes

Clouds fly into the moon
wind full of blossoms

1970

CHINESE FIGURES

Anonymous Chinese

One lifetime in office
the next seven lives a beggar

A judge decides for ten reasons
nine of which nobody knows

If you get in a fight with a tiger
call your brother

Before you beat a dog
find out whose he is

The hissing starts
in the free seats

For a whole day
he does nothing
like the immortals

If two men feed a horse
it will stay thin

Straightened too much
crooked as ever

Old man
the sun leaving
the mountain

Rank and position
gulls on water

Honor
is brought
by servants

Wear rags
and the dogs bite

Let your children
taste a little cold
and a little hunger

One word
can warm
the three months of winter

Don't insult
those in office
cheat them

The wind got up in the night
and took our plans away

So cold
the cocks crow at midnight

1969

Daio Japanese (1235–1308)

I have had a companion on the road
we have journeyed shoulder to shoulder
by nature the mountains are green
by nature the water is clear
midnight has passed
this nature is not known
all I hear
is startled monkeys above the monastery

Muso Japanese 1275–1351

For years I dug in the earth
trying to discover the blue sky
deeper and deeper I tunnelled
until one night
I made stones and tiles fly into the air
with no effort I broke the bone of the void

Takushitsu Japanese 1290–1367

A breeze strokes the water of the spring
bringing a cool sound
the moon climbs from the peak in front
lights up the bamboo window frame
With age I have found it good
to be in the heart of the mountains
To die at the foot of a cliff –
the bones would be pure forever

1977 from French versions by Masumi Shibata

Even the man who is happy
    glimpses something
    a hair of sound touches him

    and his heart overflows with a longing
        he does not recognize

then it must be that he is remembering
    in a place out of reach
    shapes he has loved

    in a life before this

    the print of them still there in him waiting

1970   translated with J. MOUSSAIEFF MASSON

I like sleeping with somebody
   different

often

it's nicest when my husband is
   in a foreign country

   and there's rain in the streets at night
   and wind

and nobody

1970   translated with J. MOUSSAIEFF MASSON

Between his hands
Krishna takes
Yasodha's breast
in his mouth takes
her nipple
at once he remembers
in an earlier life taking
to his mouth the conch shell
to call to battle
all bow down now to
the thought of his skin
at that moment

1971   tranlated with J. MOUSSAIEFF MASSON

Water pouring from clouds
in the night
of palm forests
large ears motionless
they listen
the elephants
eyes half closed
to the sound of the heavy rain
their trunks resting on their tusks

1972   translated with J. MOUSSAIEFF MASSON

Hiding in the
cucumber garden
simple country girl shivers
with desire
her lover on a low cot
lies tired with love
she melts into his body
with joy
his neck tight in her arms
one of her feet
flicking a necklace of
sea shells hanging
on a vine
on the fence
rattles them to scare off
foxes there in the dark

1973   translated with J. MOUSSAIEFF MASSON

The goddess Laksmi
loves to make love to Vishnu
from on top
looking down she sees in his navel
a lotus
and on it Brahma the god
but she can't bear to stop
so she puts her hand
over Vishnu's right eye
which is the sun
and night comes on
and the lotus closes
with Brahma inside

1973   translated with J. MOUSSAIEFF MASSON

That moon which the sky never saw
    even in dreams
    has risen again

    bringing a fire
    that no water can drown

See here where the body
    has its house
    and see here my soul

    the cup of love has made the one
    drunk
    and the other a ruin

When the tavern-keeper
    became my heart's companion

    love turned my blood
    to wine
    and my heart burned on a spit

When the eye is full of him
    a voice resounds

      Oh cup
      be praised
      oh wine be proud

That moon which the sky never saw

　　　Suddenly when my heart saw
　　　the ocean of love

　　　　it leapt away from me calling
　　　　Look for me

　　　The face of Shams-ud Din
　　　the glory of Tabriz

　　　　is the sun that hearts follow
　　　　like clouds

1974   translated with TALAT HALMAN

When the heart bursts into flame
    it swallows up
    the believers and the faithless together

      when the bird of truth
      opens its wings
      all the images fly away

The world breaks apart
    the soul is flooded

      the pearl that dissolves into water
      is embraced by the water
      and reborn from the water

The secret appears
    and the forms of the world
    fall away

      suddenly one wave
      is flung upward
      all the way to the green dome of the sky

One moment it's a pen
    one moment it's paper
    one moment it's rapture

      the soul learns to hate
      good and evil
      and keeps stabbing at both

Every soul that reaches God
enters the majestic
secret

turns from a snake
into a fish

leaves solid earth
dives into the sea
swims in the river of Paradise

The soul moves from earthly bondage
to the kingdom without place

after that wherever it falls
it is bathed in a sea of sweet odor

Absence is also
divine poverty

it guides the stars

the Emperor
turns to dust on its doorstep
knocking

Let the glittering surface
go out
so that the light within
can wake

out of the burning sun
light comes to the heart
to illumine the universe

You are in the service
    of the beloved
    why are you hiding

    you are gold
    finer and brighter
    at each stroke of the hammer

It is the heart
    that sings these words
    the wine of eternity
    has made it drunk

    but these are nothing
    to the words it would sing
    if it held its breath

1974   *translated with* TALAT HALMAN

Wise teacher tell me
    who or what do I look like

one minute I'm a phantom
    the next I call to the spirits

I stand unscorched and unshrivelled
    in the flames of longing
    and I am the candle that gives light to everything

I am the smoke and the light I am one
    and I am scattered

The one thing I ever twist in anger
    is the peg of the heart's lyre

the one thing I ever pluck
    with the plectrum
    is the harp of joy

I am like milk and honey
    I strike myself again and again
    I stop myself

when I run mad I rattle my chains

Teacher tell me what kind
    of bird am I
    neither partridge nor hawk

I'm neither beautiful nor ugly
    neither this nor that

I'm neither the pedlar in the market
    nor the nightingale
    in the rose garden

Teacher give me a name so that I'll know
    what to call myself

I'm neither slave nor free neither candle
    nor iron

I've not fallen in love with anyone
    nor is anyone in love with me

Whether I'm sinful or good
    sin and goodness come from another
    not from me

Wherever He drags me I go
    with no say in the matter

1977   translated with TALAT HALMAN

Love you alone have been with us
    since before the beginning of the world

tell us all the secrets one by one
    we are of the same Household as you

In dread of your fire we closed our mouths
    and gave up words

but you are not fire
    you are without flames

Moment by moment
    you destroy the city of the mind

gust of wind to the mind's candle
    wine for the fire-worshippers

Friend with friends
    enemy with enemies

or somewhere between the two
    looking for both

To the sane
    the words of lovers are nothing but stories

if that was all you were
    how could you turn night into day

You whose beauty sends the world reeling
    your love brings about all this confusion

You are that love's masterpiece
    you make it clear

Oh sun of God
    sultan of sultans
      glory and joy of Tabriz

you give light to those on earth
    beauty and splendor of the age

1977 translated with TALAT HALMAN

If you're not going to sleep
   sit up
   I've already slept

go on and tell your story
   I've finished mine

I've finished that story
   because I'm tired

lurching the way drunks do
   staggering
   ready to pass out

Asleep or awake
   I'm thirsty
   for the beloved

my companion
   my cherished friend
   is the image
   of the beloved

Like the mirror
   I exist only because
   of that face

for whose sake
   I display features
   or hide them

When the image of the beloved smiles
    I smile
    when the image stirs and rages with passion

I stir and rage too
    with passion
    I too let go

For the rest
    why don't you
    tell it
    you

each of the pearls
    after all
    that I'm piercing and stringing together

    came out of your sea

1977   *translated with* TALAT HALMAN

The whole universe is full of God
    yet His truth is seen by no one
    you have to look for Him in yourself
    you and he are not separate you are one

The other world is what can't be seen
    here on earth we must live as well as we can
    exile is grieving and anguish
    no one comes back who has once gone

Come let us be friends this one time
    let life be our friend
    let us be lovers of each other
    the earth will be left to no one

You know what Yunus is saying
    its meaning is in the ear of your heart
    we should all live truly here
    for we will not live here forever

1977   translated with TALAT HALMAN

GHAZAL V

Mirza Ghalib   Urdu   1797—1869

The drop dies in the river
of its joy
pain goes so far it cures itself

in the spring after the heavy rain the cloud
disappears
that was nothing but tears

in the spring the mirror turns green
holding a miracle
Change the shining wind

the rose led us to our eyes

let whatever is be open

1968   translated with AIJAZ AHMAD

GHAZAL XII

Mirza Ghalib   Urdu   1797—1869

I am not a flower of song
    nor any of the bright shuttles of music
I am the sound of my own breaking

You think of how your hair looks
I think of the ends of things

We think we know our own minds
but our hearts are children

Now that you have appeared to me I bow
may you be blessed

You look after the wretched
no wonder you came
    looking for me

1968   translated with AIJAZ AHMAD

GHAZAL XXXIV

Mirza Ghalib   Urdu   1797—1869

He's going around with your letter
showing
would be happy to read it out

Kind as she is she's made so fine
I'd be afraid to touch her
if she'd let me

Death will come whether I wait for her or not
I ask you to come whether I want you
or not

The vision
hangs before the Divine like a curtain
whose is it

Helpless with the fire of love
Ghalib
can't light it can't put it out

1968   translated with AIJAZ AHMAD

GHAZAL XXV

Mirza Ghalib   Urdu   1797—1869

If it ever occurs to her to be kind to me
she remembers how cruel she's been
and it frightens her off

Her temper's as short as my tale of love is long
much too long
bores even the messenger

and I despair
and lose the thread of my own thoughts

and can't bear to think of someone else
setting eyes on her

1968   translated with AIJAZ AHMAD

GHAZAL XXI

Mirza Ghalib   Urdu   1797—1869

Red poppy
    a heart
    an eye

      one dewdrop on it
      a tear

      there to hide something

      she is cruel
      it leaves its mark

But the scar of the burnt heart
    oh my cry
    is nothing

      beside you oh my cry
      dove
      turned to ashes
      nightingale
      prison of color

No blaze of meeting
    could have burned like the longing to meet

      the spirits were consumed
      the heart suffered torture

If a man claims to be a prisoner of love
he is a prisoner of something
hand held down by a stone
faithful

Oh sun
you light the whole world
here also
shine

a strange time has come over us
like a shadow

1968 translated with AIJAZ AHMAD

GHAZAL XV

Mirza Ghalib   Urdu   1797—1869

Almost none
of the beautiful faces
come back to be glimpsed for an instant in some flower

once the dust owns them

The three Daughters of the Bier
as becomes stars
hide in the light till day has gone

then they step forth naked
but their minds are the black night

He is the lord of sleep
lord of peace
lord of night

on whose arm your hair is lying

1968   translated with AIJAZ AHMAD

W. S. Merwin was born in New York City in 1927 and grew up in Union City, New Jersey, and in Scranton, Pennsylvania. From 1949 to 1951 he worked as a tutor in France, Portugal, and Majorca. After that, for several years he made the greater part of his living by translating from French, Spanish, Latin and Portuguese. Since 1954 several fellowships have been of great assistance. In addition to poetry, he has written articles, chiefly for *The Nation*, and radio scripts for the BBC. He has lived in England, France, and the United States. His books of poetry are *A Mask for Janus* (1952), *The Dancing Bears* (1954), *Green with Beasts* (1956), *The Drunk in the Furnace* (1960) (available in one volume as *The First Four Books of Poems*), *The Moving Target* (1963), *The Lice* (1967), *The Carrier of Ladders* (1970) for which he received the Pulitzer Prize, *Writings to an Un-finished Accompaniment* (1973) and *The Compass Flower* (1977). An earlier book of prose, *The Miner's Pale Children*, was published in 1970. His translations include *The Poem of the Cid* (1959), *Spanish Ballads* (1960), *The Satires of Persius* (1961), *Lazarillo de Tormes* (1962), *The Song of Roland* (1963), *Selected Translations 1948–1968* (1968) for which he won the P.E.N. Translation Prize for 1968, *Transparence of the World*, a translation of his selection of poems by Jean Follain (1969), (with Clarence Brown) *Osip Mandel-stam, Selected Poems* (1974), (with George E. Dimock, Jr.) *Iphigeneia at Aulis* by Euripedes (1977), (with J. Moussaieff Masson) *Classical Sanskrit Love Poetry* (1977) and *Vertical Poetry* a translation of his selection of poems by Roberto Juarroz (1977). In 1974 he was awarded The Fellowship of the Academy of American Poets.